Video Marketing for Veterinarians

7 Marketing Strategies to Attract New Clients

By Michelle Duplechan
and
Jenn Foster

Video Marketing for Veterinarians

7 Marketing Strategies to Attract New Clients

©2015,
Duplechan Marketing Solutions
1467 Monte Verde Avenue
Upland, CA, 91786
Phone: (626) 221-8024
E-mail:michelleduplechan@gmail.com

Biz Social Boom
63 East 11400 South, #230
Draper, UT 84070
Phone: (801) 901-3480
E-mail:jenn@bizsocialboom.com

Register This Book and Get

Free Updates and Free Videos

To get updates to this book and access to FREE informative videos that will show you how to attract new clients with videos, visit www.VeterinarianVideoMarketingBook.com, you can also text your email address to 1 (909) 570-1605 or scan this QR Code:

Table of Contents

About the Authors:

Michelle Duplechan is dedicated to helping your business grow by combining various online and offline methods. Her company Duplechan Marketing Solutions will bring more qualified leads through your door and help you build relationships with your prospects and customers. By using powerful tools such as online video and automated systems to capture leads and follow up with them automatically, she will help to create trust with your prospects and clients and keep them coming back to you over and over again. She is also the host of The Moms in Business Talk Show, a podcast show dedicated to moms who own their own businesses where they share the joys and challenges of raising their children while building their businesses, as well as give encouragement and helpful tips and resources. When she is not helping clients, Michelle enjoys spending time with her 2 teenage daughters, reading, hiking, and working out. Additional information about Michelle and her business can be found at www.dmstoday.com.

Follow Michelle at:

Facebook: www.facebook.com/michelle.duplechan

YouTube: www.youtube.com/user/DMSToday

Jenn Foster, is one of today's national leading online and mobile marketing experts. She is the founder and CEO of Biz Social Boom, a company dedicated to helping business owners of all sizes thrive in today's highly technical world of product and service promotion. From local brick and mortar stores to online entities and to large international corporations, Jenn's years of experience and expertise has helped hundreds of others become the front page news on all of the major search engines. She is dedicated to helping businesses use powerful new online and mobile marketing platforms to get visibility, traffic, leads, customers and raving fans.

A graduate of Utah State University, Jenn is an award winning web designer, author, and sought after speaker. She has been a featured speaker at such events as the Kim Flynn's Internet Marketing Boot Camp, Utah Crowd-

Funding Association and the Sandy Area Chamber of Commerce among others. She has been on stage as an expert marketing panelist for marketing experts Mike Koenigs, Ed Rush, Paul Colligan and Pam Hendrickson. She was also an expert guest on the Teach Jim Show on Blog Talk Radio. Jenn has been a guest on multiple podcast shows including: Instant Authority Expert with Keith Shannon, Stephanie Bavaro's Greatful Women Talks, Online Marketing Guy Livecast by Steven Laurvick, The Moms in Business Talk Show with Michelle Duplechan and many more. Jenn has been named one of America's Premier Experts® and is a co-author in the book Stand Apart with Dan Kennedy, a major national publication, and an Amazon kindle best seller. Jenn recently received a Quilly Award in Hollywood from the National Academy of Best Selling Authors, for her contribution to the book.

Coming from a family of successful entrepreneurs, Jenn grew up around thriving businesses and understands what it takes to create, run and promote winning companies from the ground up. Combining her education, knowledge and life-long experience, today Jenn teaches people and businesses globally how they can get found in today's virtual world, how they can engage prospects on their terms and how to continue to connect and follow up with prospects to convert them to customers. By utilizing her proven techniques, Jenn confidently guarantees her clients will be on the first page of Google Search in their local market.

When she is not helping her clients, Jenn enjoys spending time with her three children, sewing with her family 4-H club, experiencing the great outdoors and she loves Zumba. Additional information about Jenn and her business can be found at www.JennFosterSEO.net or by texting your email to **(801) 901-3480**.

Follow Jenn at:

Facebook: www.FaceBook.com/JennFosterChic

Twitter: @JennFosterChic

YouTube: www.YouTube.com/user/VideoFacebook101/

Other Books by Jenn Foster:

Stand Apart: Stand Out From the Crowd to Achieve Ultimate Success.
Featuring Dan Kennedy, Jenn Foster and Leading Experts From Around the World.

Video and Social Media Marketing for Professionals: The Top 10 Need to Know Facts for Increasing Local and Internet Traffic

Special Thanks to

From Michelle:

The One who holds my very breath in the palm of His hand.

My 2 daughters, I love you with ALL my heart and you are my "why"!

My mom, dad, sister and brother, for always being there for me no matter what.

Jenn Foster, without you, this book would not have been created. You inspire me!

Our readers. We hope that this book will help you to develop a better understanding of what this "video marketing thing" is, but more than that, inspire you to take action and start using video to grow your business.

From Jenn:

The Mike Koenigs Team, and his community of amazing leaders, experts and authors.

My 3 kids, who push me to do great things!

Our clients and customers that make it possible for us to live our dreams.

Michelle, you are an inspiration, and I'm so happy we met.

Introduction

The intention of this book is to help you become more knowledgeable about marketing your veterinary clinic using videos as well as to develop your confidence in creating videos, whether you create them yourself or hire a professional video production company to do it for you.

If you choose to hire a pro, you will gain enough foundational knowledge in this book to have an intelligent conversation with the pro. This book will also give you a better idea of how to incorporate video marketing into what you are already doing.

What this book is not about:

This is not a book about the best camera to use, the best equipment or the best video editing software you should use to create your videos.

What this book is about:

This book is about the elements you should include in your videos to make them more compelling. It is about the types of videos you should make to attract clients to your clinic, as well as video marketing strategies to get more engagement from your viewers and get your videos found so that you get the most out of the time, energy and investment.

You probably bought this book because you have at least an interest in how video marketing works and may be thinking about incorporating it into your marketing mix.

Let's start off with a question you may be asking yourself.

Will creating videos for my veterinary clinic really help me attract new clients or will I be wasting my money?

Before we answer that question, let's start with a hypothetical real world example.

Example story:

Imagine a young couple, a husband and wife, married for about a year, both animal lovers, and they would like to add a furry member to their family.

They decide they want a puppy, so they research different breeds and finally decide on a getting a Yorkie, because they are tiny and seemingly easier to care for than a larger breed.

They go to the local pet store and buy a food and water dish, dog food, a doggie bed, toys and various grooming tools, including a doggie tooth brush.

They go to the breeder, pick out their adorable little bundle of joy and bring her to their home!

Now that they have her home, there are a few things they realize they need to find out:

- When to get her shots
- What to do to keep her healthy
- How to brush her teeth
- When to get her spayed
- And a whole lot of other things!

They know they need to take her to a veterinarian they can trust, so they get into research mode, go online to Google, and look for one that is in their city.

Here is what they find:

They get a bit overwhelmed, they see a list of several veterinarians to choose from, but they can't tell one apart from the other because all the information that comes up in their search looks the same.

As a side note, there are people in your local area right now looking for the services or products that you have to offer. But when most people go online, they search for *information* and not necessarily for your specific veterinary clinic. At this point, they most likely have no idea who you are or what makes you different from any of the other veterinary clinics that show up in the search results, as you can see from the screenshot above. What they care about is finding answers to their questions or solutions to their problems.

Let us repeat that so that it really sinks in:

What people really care about is finding answers to their questions or solutions to their problems

Now what if the results they found looked like this instead?

RCC Solar: Solar Panel Installation | Home Solar Power ...
www.rccsolar.com
RCC Solar is your source for premier solar panel systems and solar panel installation services. Located in Upland, our solar power systems are among the most.
4 Google reviews · Write a review · Google+ page

- 90 East Stowell Street, Upland, CA 91786

RCC/ Restart Solar - Upland, CA | Yelp
www.yelp.com › Home Services › Solar Installation › Yelp
★★★★★ Rating 5 · 14 reviews
14 Reviews of RCC Restart Solar. My experience with RCC was great from I trust RCC completely and recommend them for your total energy solution project.

RCC Solar - SolarReviews
www.solarreviews.com/installers/rcc-solar-reviews
★★★★★ Rating 4.9 · 4 reviews
RCC Solar. 90 E Stowell St. Upland CA 91786 ... RCC Solar designs and builds the highest performing solar energy systems in the industry ... [more]. Our team

Upland Renewable Energy Products and Guarantees ...

www.youtube.com/watch?vrz5sRqdNsWKU
Feb 6, 2014 - Uploaded by Restart Solar
Upland Renewable Energy http://www.rccsolar.com We have installed solar on over 250 homes in the Inland.

Upland CA 91784 Solar Power Solar Energy
solarenergyexchange.net/upland-ca-91784-solar-power-solar-energy.php
Solar Power in Upland - Solar Energy Exchange. Air Conditioning and Refrigeration Inc. provides air conditioner, air cleaner, air filter

Upland family get free solar panels through new partnership
www.dailybulletin.com › upland-family-get › inland valley Daily Bulletin
May 2, 2015 - UPLAND - The Zavala family in Upland recently benefitted from a new partnership between GRID Alternatives and Sullivan Solar Power.

Rancho Cucamonga Website - Solar - Cityofrc.us
www.cityofrc.us › Healthy Earth › City of Rancho Cucamonga
Converting energy from the sun is a clean, renewable, and economical way to power homes and buildings. Solar energy is great for homeowners, businesses.

RCC Solar Inc | Upland, CA 91786 | Angies List
www.angieslist.com › Local Reviews › Upland › Angies List
Services: Solar Panels. In Business Since: 2006. Service Area: San Bernardino County, Orange County, Los Angeles County, Riverside County, Upland.

Solar Energy in CA
www.sungevity.com/free-quote
As Low As $0 Down & Free Install. No-Hassle Quote From Solar Experts

SunPower® Solar Panels
www.sunpower.com
Most Efficient Residential Solar Panels Under The Sun. Go Solar

Affordable Home Electric
www.solarcity.com
★★★★★ Rating for solarcity.com
Custom Solar Power Systems to Lower Your Electric Bill. Get a Quote!

Solar Energy For Home
www.greenpowersolarpanels.com/Energy
$0 Down & Free Installation. Visit Our WebSite & Get Free Energy Quote

Upland Solar Install
www.modernize.com/Cheapest-Solar
★★★★★ Rating for modernize.com
$0 Down. Save 80% on Electric Bill. Local Federal Rebates Ending Soon.

Solar Energy For Homes
www.solarforzerodown.com
$0 Down Home Solar Power Companies Free Home Solar Electric Analysis!

See your ad here »

The example shown here is for a different industry, but which result stands out to you? Where is the eye automatically drawn to? And be honest...which result are you most likely to check out first if you were looking to add solar energy panels to your home?

22

As you can see, the video thumbnail stands out from all the other search results and, as research has shown, most people would rather watch information than read it. Most people do not want to read through a lot of text, but they would gladly sit for a minute or two to watch a video.

This means that you will effectively be taking business AWAY from your competitors.

Back to our story:

As the couple is searching for a veterinarian in their city, they come across your video in the search results. They click on it first because their eye is drawn to it, they watch the video, get to see and hear you, and get to know a little about your personality. In essence, they get to "meet" you before actually seeing you in person.

After they watch your video, they notice you have other helpful videos that answer other questions they have, like how to groom their puppy and how to brush her teeth. They watch the videos where they can see how to do it, rather than reading about it in an article.

Before you know it, they have watched 2 or 3 of your videos, and without them probably even realizing it, have started to "know, like, and trust" you because you are freely sharing the information they are looking for.

If you are the only veterinary clinic standing out in the search results, and you are answering the questions or challenges this couple is looking for answers to, maybe even giving the viewers of your video an incentive, such as a 20% discount for first-time patients, who do you think they are most likely to call and set up an appointment with for their adorable little Yorkie?

After reading this hypothetical, but real-life story that happens every day, how would you now answer the question we posed before?

"Will creating videos for my veterinary clinic really help me attract new clients or will I be wasting my money?"

By the way, the vast majority of potential clients in your local area surfing the web are probably not in the mood to make an appointment or purchase anything from you right away. Instead, they want information on what you have to offer.

You most likely have pages and pages of text on your website designed to educate somebody about your services, but most people do not want to read through that information. People are hungry for informative content, but they would much rather digest that information in easy to watch videos.

Before we get into the 7 simple strategies to attract new clients, let's talk a bit about...

The power and benefits of online video:

- Excellent for branding. You are perceived as the authority and "go to" expert in your local area because you stand out and are marketing your clinic differently than 99% of all the other veterinarians in your city or area

- Develops that "know, like & trust" factor that is so very important to help you attract more clients to your clinic making it much easier to sell your products and services. What the "know, like & trust" is really about is this: people want to know what they are getting themselves into before they part with their cash

- You can engage with, and start to build relationships with people, and as trust grows, you become the obvious choice for prospective clients to take their pets to - trust and credibility are absolutely everything
- It can work for your veterinary clinic, over and over again and year after year, gaining new prospects and clients along the way, as long as you are teaching, helping and providing valuable information. You create a video one time, and it keeps working for you
- The video will help drive QUALIFIED traffic to your website, blog, lead capture page, or anywhere you want to send traffic to
- It provides the opportunity to put your business in front of hundreds or even thousands of people – whether in your local area or worldwide which is like having a sales army working for you 24/7... even while you're sleeping!
- Say more in less time. If a picture is worth 1,000 words, then a video must be worth 1.8 million

words! There are things that you can convey in a video which you simply would not be able to convey in text no matter how hard you try

- A video is personal, engaging, intimate and has a powerful "connection factor"
- Helps with online lead generation
- It can be used for event promotions. If you have any special events you hold at your clinic for your patients and clients, be sure to create a short video about it and share it all over using social media
- The bottom line - video helps you make more sales

One extra HUGE benefit: just one video can be turned into various types of media, also known as "repurposing," which expands your reach even more:

- Articles – a transcript of your video can be turned into an article and submitted to article directories such as www.ezinearticles.com and www.goarticles.com

- Images – screen shots from your video can be taken and posted to image sharing sites such as Pinterest and Instagram
- Social media – a thumbnail of your video with links to it can be posted to social media sites such as Facebook, Twitter and LinkedIn
- Mp3's – an audio file of your video can be posted to places like iTunes
- PDFs – the transcription and graphics/images from your video can be made into an e-book that you can make available online
- Kindle books – the transcription and graphics/ images from your video can be made into a Kindle book, making you a published author on Amazon!
- You can create CDs and DVDs
- And the list goes on...

You may not have a desire to do any of these things at this time, but the options are there if you ever decide to do at least one of them. You invest time, energy and money when you create a video, so you may as well get the most out of it by repurposing your content.

"Creativity is intelligence having fun." – Albert Einstein

Video Marketing Strategy #1

- Types of videos to make:

There are many choices about what types of videos to make. The type you make depends on the goal of the video, but for now, here are a few suggestions that would be excellent to use for your veterinary clinic:

- Videos that answer questions and/or solve a problem – FAQs & SAQs
- Client testimonials
- "How to" videos
- About Us video
- Home page video
- Product demos

- Product reviews
- Review videos
- Video tips series

FAQs – Frequently Asked Questions

What questions do you notice that your clients are constantly asking? What problems can you solve for them? These are questions you find yourself answering over and over again.

You can make separate videos answering each of those questions.

Here are 10 sample FAQ questions. Of course, you may have a totally different set of questions that you get asked frequently, so just use this as an example:

- What can I expect on my first visit to your clinic?
- At what age can I spay or neuter my pet?
- Can I feed my dog bones (pork chop bones, steak bones, chicken bones)?
- How do I brush my dog's teeth?
- My dog ate poison. What should I do?

- What is the best natural flea remedy?

- What can I do about my dog/cat's bad breath?

- I think my dog has worms, what should I do? Can I or my children get worms from my dog/cat?

- My cat has ear mites. How frequently must it be treated and for how long?

- How can I stop my dog from eating its own feces?

Make sure that each video has valuable, relevant content so that people who are searching for answers to their questions will find and watch your videos to the end. Also, make the majority of your videos two minutes or less, and make sure you focus only on a single point.

For example, if you are making a video about "how to brush my dog's teeth," then keep the video on that topic only. Better to make one point with impact than confuse your viewer with information overload.

SAQs: - Should Ask Questions

What questions do you feel your prospects and clients SHOULD ask you but simply don't know enough to ask?

These are the kinds of questions you wish they would ask that differentiate you from the other veterinary clinics in your city.

Make videos based on aspects that make you stand out from your competition – something you do that others don't do OR that you know you do better, such as maybe you have the latest technological equipment to detect illness before others do.

Of course these questions would differ depending on what your clinic has to offer.

Here are 5 sample SAQ questions:

- Do you have an in-house lab to get results quickly?
- Do you treat exotic animals, such as reptiles?

- Do you separate cats from dogs in the waiting room so the environment is more stress-free for the patients?
- Do you provide payment plans?
- Do you provide workshops or classes on how best to care for my pet?

You could always answer the FAQs and SAQs in text form and just put them on your website. However, why not do something different? Why not give that answer a bit more of a personal touch? The benefit is that your viewers and clients feel 'special', and you are also producing good quality content that can be shared.

Client testimonials:

Client testimonials are SOCIAL PROOF, which in this day & age has a huge impact. A very large percentage of people go online looking for reviews of businesses they are considering doing business with, and if you have stories of your happy clients on video, catching their excitement on camera to be seen and heard, that has a much greater impact on the viewer than simply reading text on a page. You should upload these videos to your website and YouTube.

Another benefit is they provide more value to prospective clients when they're on the fence about calling you to make an appointment.

Do NOT pay for video testimonials. People can tell if somebody is being truthful or not. Only use real clients of yours. People love something that sounds natural, and no, actors do not sound natural.

Below is a template for the "Perfect Customer Testimonial" to help you get the most out of your testimonials - provided by Mike Koenigs at Instant Customer

The Perfect Testimonial Template:

You may want to go over the questions with them in advance to get them comfortable and help them prepare for the actual video recording.

"My name is _____, I'm from

_____.

[name] [city] [state]

I _____ for

_____.

[profession/what you do] [who you do it for]

_____

_____

[Expose a personal weakness, challenge, pain or loss - for example:*"Ever* since_____ / I'm not good at _____ / I'm experiencing

_____ / major pain or challenge."]

_____

_____

[Describe how things have been: *losing money, wasting
time, never seeing my kids, working too much, affecting
my health*]

_____

_____

[Describe your major discovery - and what happened:
e.g. "*I bought my house and now I can own it for less
than I paid in rent!*"]
[Describe how things are now, how much more money
you're saving, more
house, - BE SPECIFIC]

_____

_____

[How will <Your New Home> change your income,
business, free time, your
health, your family or your ability to contribute to a
higher cause?

_____

_____

[Bonus: what do your spouse/kids/friends/co-workers/ peers say? Example: *"My kids are so happy they love the backyard and the new neighbors"*]

_____

_____

[Closing: "Thank you, (Company), for (BIG BENEFIT) *"Thank you, (Company)*, for <mention big benefit here.> OR "Thanks, (Company) for helping me save more money and giving me the home I've always dreamed of. I never thought I could do it or even qualify for a loan, but I'm living proof that if I can do it, you can do it too."]

_____

_____

*©Mike Koenigs - Instant Customer

"How to" videos:

This is pretty self-explanatory. Create videos about how to do something.

People generally go to the internet to find information about how to do things, so if you provide the answers they are looking for, you are that much closer to getting another new client.

One reason why "how to" videos work so well is that they can help people quickly and easily understand how a product or service works. Some studies suggest that people's understanding of a product increased by 74% after watching a video. A better understanding of the product meant that they could make a much more informed decision when purchasing.

In a video, you can demonstrate exactly how your product or service works. In just a couple of minutes of watching a video, people will have a much better understanding of what you are all about and how you can help them.

Examples of a few "how to" videos for your veterinary clinic might be:

- how to properly brush my dog's teeth
- how to clean my cat's ears
- how to properly apply flea medication
- the best way to bathe my dog
- how to properly administer oral medication
- how to trim my pet's nails

There are a number of problems that people are looking to solve on a daily basis. Why not show off your knowledge and help them solve them? Just a quick 'step by step' of how to solve a problem without selling your product or service. This will go a long way in building trust and credibility with your viewers.

About us video:

When you use a video on the "About Us" page of your website, you have a powerful opportunity to:

- Bring your story to life
- Engage with your viewers on a deeper level

You can openly share:

- "Why" – the reason you do what you do. Why did you become a veterinarian? Was it a dream of yours as a child? Did something happen to a pet of yours that made you want to become a

veterinarian? What is the story behind that?

- Passion
- Struggles

****

Tell me a fact and I remember.

Tell me a truth and I believe.

Tell me a story and I hold it in my heart forever...

****

When people know who you are and why you do what you do at a deeper level, every additional video you create has much more power and engagement behind it.

Home Page video:

Having a video on the home page of your website is a great way to immediately grab the attention of your visitors and keep their attention on your website.

It's a known fact that visitors stay much longer on a website with a video than on one without a video.

Your home page video should be about 3 simple things:

- who you are
- what you do – keeping what you can do for the client in mind
- why you are different – keeping what you can do for the client in mind

This should be a fairly short video, generally no longer than a minute to a minute and a half.

People are naturally more interested in what you can do for them and their pets, so make this video more about them than about you directly.

Creating this type of video helps your clients know, like and trust you. When they understand who you are, what you can do for them, and why you are different than other veterinary clinics, they will want to call you and make an appointment.

Creating trust is crucial for doing business online, and there's no quicker way to establish rapport than with video.

Product demos and/or product reviews:

- Product demos - making videos demonstrating your products and services is easy! You know your own products and showing others the best ways to use them or why they should choose your service over someone else's is a great way to get started. It is much easier to demonstrate exactly what something can do in a video, and much more enjoyable for the viewer, as opposed to reading plain text

- Product reviews – people are always looking for product and service reviews online. If you can create videos that are helpful to your prospects and clients, they will be more likely to call you or visit your veterinary office to get the product

****

If you can't explain it to a 6-year old,

you don't know it yourself

– Albert Einstein

****

Examples of a service demo video could be:

- you demonstrating how friendly your staff is when people bring in their pets
- what you do to make the patient comfortable in the room while they are waiting for the doctor
- the way you do a pet exam

Examples of a product demo could be:

- you demonstrating a super easy way to apply a particular flea medication on their pet
- you demonstrating an ear cleaning solution
- a pet food

And of course, these would all be products that you have for sale there in your office!

As a doctor of veterinary medicine, you can turn your wisdom, advice, knowledge, experience and expertise into videos which will eventually bring more clients to your office.

Review videos:

Review videos are different from client testimonial videos, but are just as important.

When potential clients are making the decision as to whether to make an appointment with you or not, it is likely they will look up reviews online first. After all, they want to know that you will take excellent care of their family pet and that their money is going to be well-spent.

Review videos are basically slide show videos that contain some of your best online reviews from sites like Yelp and any of the other online review sites. Since people will be leaving you reviews in text form on the review sites, you may as well use them to your advantage by creating a video out of them.

When you create the title for your review videos, you need to include your clinic name as well as the word "reviews" and the city you are in.

Here is an example title for a review video:

"San Bernardino Pet Hospital Reviews – San Bernardino, CA Animal Hospital"

You simply take 5-7 of your best online reviews and put them in a slide show with some music and your contact information, that way when people are looking for reviews of your veterinary clinic, they see your video, which they are more likely to click on.

Video tips series:

Creating a series of videos on a particular topic is a powerful way to position yourself as the expert on that topic in your area.

For example, you could create a video series on "all things dogs" – dental care, disease prevention, spay/neuter after care, grooming, exercise, flea prevention, heart-worm prevention, etc.

As a veterinarian, you have a wealth of information to share. Create a series of short videos on various topics, about two minutes or less each, and very soon you will have several online videos all working for you and pointing your viewers right to you.

****

A year from now, you'll wish you had started today

– Karen Lamb

****

Video Marketing Strategy #2
- Look and feel of your video:

This strategy is where you decide what kind of video you are going to create.

Here are a few options for you to look at, and each one will create a different look and feel as a representation of your veterinary clinic:

Talking head video – this is where you, one of your employees or a hired actor stands or sits and speaks while looking directly into the camera. If the person in front of the camera looks directly at the lens, rather than reading a script from a teleprompter, it looks like they are making direct eye contact with the viewer of the video - the best thing next to a face-to-face meeting.

Off-camera interview style – this is where the person in front of the camera looks off to the side of the camera as though speaking with someone else. This is a good option for those who are uncomfortable with looking directly at a camera lens.

Here are 2 options for those who really do not want to be in front of the camera:

Animated – animated videos have become extremely popular in the last year, and even in television commercials. There are different styles to choose from, including cartoon animation and whiteboard animation videos.

These animated videos, also referred to as explainer videos, can be extremely effective when done right. The fact that they are animated in no way diminishes the impact they can have for your veterinary clinic. They tend to be very eye-catching and keep people's attention.

Animated videos could be used to give a breakdown of the services that your veterinary clinic offers and how they benefit the client and/or patient. They are so versatile that they can also be used to provide your viewers with helpful information, such as advice and tips. Just remember to keep them short and simple.

Slide show – this is where you put together a slide show of pictures and even short video clips, with some text, music and possibly a voice over.

You will want to add music to whichever style of video you choose to create. The right music can completely change the mood and feel of your video, and you want to be sure to match the music to the feel you want in your video. Be sure to keep the volume of the music down so that it stays in the background and doesn't drown out your voice or a voice over if you're doing an animated or slide show video.

Imagine watching a high energy video about people surfing in the ocean while Chopin's Funeral March is playing in the background...talk about a mismatch of music to video content!

****

Humans are incredibly visual and powerful, moving images help us find meaning...and video helps capture and contextualize the world around us
- Dan Patterson

****

Video Marketing Strategy #3
- Elements to include in your videos:

1 - Every video needs to have a goal or intention.

Before you create any videos, you need to decide what the purpose of the video is. Do not waste your time creating videos without having a specific purpose in mind.

Is it to get people to call you? Is it to get people to come in to your clinic and redeem a coupon or special offer? To subscribe to your YouTube channel? Or to get more Facebook likes on your business page?

It is one thing to create a video and put it out there, but it's another to create a video that actually works for you. A video that actually converts and inspires a person to take the next step with you, which brings us to our next element...

2 - Every video you create MUST have a call-to-action!

A call-to-action is simply letting the viewer know what you want them to do after watching your video...and be specific.

Some examples are to:

- buy your product or service
- subscribe to your YouTube channel
- opt-in to your newsletter
- like your Facebook page
- call a phone number
- click a link
- send you an email
- redeem a coupon
- or whatever step you would like them to take next with you

If you don't have some sort of call-to-action in each video, you are wasting your time and money. If you don't tell people what to do after watching your video, they will simply click away, move on to something else and likely forget about you, and once that happens, you've lost an opportunity to connect with that potential client.

* *

If you aim at nothing, you will hit it every time

– Zig Ziglar

* *

Video Marketing Strategy #4
- Ask questions:

It is important to ask a question at the end of your video that is relevant to the content of the video. Asking for feedback is a great way to get your viewers to comment and interact with you.

Generally, people who like to talk will comment on your video with or without you asking them to do so, but asking a question or soliciting feedback, opinions or stories, will encourage those who normally would not do it.

Be sure to ask open-ended questions that encourage a dialog rather than a simple "yes" or "no" answer. Also, stick to one question or one topic you would like them to talk about, so you can keep the conversation focused.

If it isn't appropriate to ask a question, ask them to share an experience they have had in relation to the content of your video.

For example, let's say you created a video about how to keep ticks away from your dog when hiking in the mountains. You can ask your viewers to share an experience they had when their dog got ticks.

When you get people answering your question or commenting on your video, be sure to respond to them, as this makes it an interactive experience and creates even more of a relationship with your viewers, who then have a greater chance of becoming your client. They also see that there is a "real person" that is responding to them and it builds that trust and relationship once again.

****

Marketing is no longer about the stuff that you make,

but about the stories you tell – Seth Godin

****

Video Marketing Strategy #5
- Where to post your videos for
social engagement:

One of the best ways to get exposure and develop relationships with people is through social media.

If you are providing helpful relevant information in an engaging or entertaining way, people will share your videos with their friends, giving you even more exposure.

Below is a short list of places to post your videos to get maximum engagement. It is by no means an exhaustive list, rather a list to get you thinking about the possibilities.

- YouTube

- Vimeo

- Social media- Facebook, Google +, LinkedIn, Pinterest, Instagram, a link to your video on Twitter

- Your website or blog

- Email campaigns

We'll delve a little more into each of these.

YouTube – Google owns YouTube and YouTube is the 2nd largest search engine in the world. It's the place where millions of people go each month to find out information, be inspired and be entertained.

It's FREE to upload your videos to YouTube, and you can upload as many videos as you want. One of the best parts is that the traffic is already there, you don't have to go looking for it, so it's kind of like going fishing where you know the fish already are.

Vimeo – Vimeo is a site where you can have your videos hosted, and you can also watch and share videos. If you are creating videos for business, you will need to get the paid version.

Social media sites – Sharing your videos on a social media platform is one of the best ways to get engagement on them. Share them on every platform you are on, including Facebook, Google+, LinkedIn, Pinterest, Instagram and even a link to your video on Twitter.

Your website or blog – Your website or blog is the "online home" of your veterinary clinic. Embed your videos on your site or blog so that when people land there, they will get the opportunity to get to know you and see the value you provide.

Email campaigns – You can include links to your videos right from the body of your email newsletter. Ask your subscribers to watch them and possibly even like and comment on them.

****

Online video is no longer a luxury, it is a necessity

****

Video Marketing Strategy #6
- Publishing consistency & frequency:

The difference between consistency and frequency:

Consistency is the "when" you publish new videos, such as the first Monday of every month, or Tuesday of every week.

Frequency refers to the number of videos you publish within a certain time frame, such as 1 video per month, or 2 videos per week.

THE KEY is this - you want to add new content on a regular basis, whether it is once a week or once a month. However often you decide to publish your videos, which we recommend no less than once a month, be sure to stick to that schedule.

You can even create several videos in one day, which is the most time-efficient way to do it, and release at predetermined times. For example, share your videos on

Tuesday of every week, or on the first Monday of each month.

The more video content you create and publish online, the more people will see it, and the more clients you will attract to your clinic.

****

Do or do not; there is no try

— Yoda

****

Video Marketing Strategy #7
- How to get your videos found
- video SEO:

This strategy is last, but certainly not least.

You put time, money and energy into creating videos, but it won't help you at all if no one ever finds them, right?

In this section, we will be talking about using YouTube to host your videos, and how to position your videos so that they are found in both the Google search results and the YouTube search results.

This topic could be a separate book in itself, and changes whenever Google decides to make changes to their algorithms, but there are some basic, foundational techniques that work no matter what changes they make.

The reason for this is that Google wants to provide the people that search on their platform with the best and most relevant content, so if you get the following elements right, you are well on your way to reaping the rewards of all the work you put into your videos.

Here is a list of some foundational techniques you need to do to optimize your videos and increase their online visibility:

Title – the title is extremely important, because your title determines if people will find your video and if they will click on it. It needs to briefly express what the content of the video is about, with the most important keywords at the beginning of the title.

Here is a quote directly from the YouTube site – "Titles help audiences and YouTube's discovery systems make sense of your content, so be sure to include relevant keywords that help describe your content."

- Example title #1: Can My Dog Eat Bones? | Veterinary Hospital San Bernardino
- Example title #2: Veterinary Clinic San Bernardino | San Bernardino Vet (555)-555-5555

Titles can be in the form of a question or as a statement. If someone has a question, they generally type that question directly into a search engine, and if they are looking for something more specific, for example a veterinary clinic in San Bernardino, or an Italian restaurant in Los Angeles, they will type that in.

*As a side note, keywords are simply descriptive words that people type into the search engines when they are looking for information, as in the examples above.

Some example keywords that could be used for a veterinary clinic or hospital: veterinary, veterinary medicine, veterinary clinic, veterinary surgery, veterinary hospital, veterinary services, veterinary surgeon, veterinary advice, veterinary clinics, pet hospital, animal hospital

Example keywords to use for your local area: veterinary hospital San Bernardino, veterinary medicine San Bernardino, veterinary surgery San Bernardino, veterinary hospital San Bernardino, veterinary services San Bernardino, veterinary surgeon San Bernardino, veterinary advice San Bernardino, veterinary clinics San Bernardino, pet hospital San Bernardino, animal hospital San Bernardino

Description : the description of your video should provide a detailed overview of the content of the video. It helps your viewers to understand what they'll be watching, and also plays a large role in video SEO.

The keywords you have chosen to use in your title should be included in the first part of the description as well.

Here is a direct quote from the YouTube site regarding descriptions – "Only the first few sentences of your video description will appear in search results and above the fold on a watch page - so make them count!"

Here is a screen shot of what they are referring to:

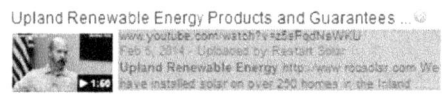

Be sure to add the link to your website at the beginning of your description with the http:// in front of it to make a clickable link. Add your phone number within the first two lines or your call to action.

Example description of a video about how to brush your dog's teeth:

> http://www.yourwebsite.com Brushing your dog's teeth may actually prevent some serious canine health problems. In this video, we learn the proper technique for brushing your dog's teeth, how often you should brush your dog's teeth, and other home care options to keep your dog's teeth healthy.
>
> For more information you can contact us at:
>
> San Bernardino Pet Clinic
>
> 1234 Doggie Lane
>
> San Bernardino, CA
>
> (555) 555-5555

Tags – there is a place on YouTube when you upload your video, to include "tags". These are words that are relevant to what your video is about, and you can also include words that have to do with your location.

Do not go overboard on the tags – 5-10 is good.

Examples of tags for your veterinary clinic could be:

- How to brush a dog's teeth
- Canine dental health
- Veterinarian clinic San Bernardino
- Pet hospital San Bernardino
- Veterinary clinic San Bernardino

There are other steps to take to best optimize your videos, but it is not within the scope of this book to cover each and every step. These are foundational steps to take that will get you off to a great start!

Now that we have covered the 7 simple strategies to attract more clients, we are going to get into other techniques that will help you create engaging videos for your veterinary clinic.

Here are 4 things to keep in mind when creating any kind of video:

1. Always add value – the viewer should come away from your video feeling like it actually helped them in some way – they either learned something or were entertained...better yet...both!
2. Keep them relevant – stick with the title and topic of your video
3. Make them consistently – better to make 1 video a week than to do ten at one time and then nothing for six months. Even better would be to create several videos in one day and then release them on a consistent basis

4. Focus on serving your clients and filling a need or solving a pain – VERY important point. Always keep your client's needs in mind when you are deciding what topic to create a video on

If using video to attract new clients to your veterinary clinic can be so beneficial, why is it that doctors hesitate?

Here are a few thoughts:

- Don't know what to make videos about
- They focus on the "what" instead of the "how"
- Think it is cost prohibitive
- Perfectionism

<u>Don't know what to make videos about</u> - as previously discussed in this book, there are several things you can make videos about. Actually, the only limit is your imagination.

Besides the previous suggestions, you can also make videos about:

Behind the scenes – create a video showing places of your clinic people don't normally get to see. Maybe you can include the room where you do the surgeries, where you keep the animals in the back, etc.

Conduct short interviews of each of the doctors and staff, or have each staff member introduce themselves and what they do at the clinic

They focus on the "what" instead of the "how" – the "what" is the technical stuff like "What kind of camera do I need?", "What kind of lighting?" or "What kind of file extension do I need to use?"

Do not let technology be the reason you don't create videos.

The "how" is where the $$ is made. – "How am I going to attract new clients?", "How am I going to drive traffic to my website?" or "How am I going to use this video to increase sales?"

Don't let the "what" get in the way of creating videos to grow your veterinary practice. If it seems overwhelming, you can always hire a video production team to do it all for you.

They think it is cost prohibitive - a television commercial for your veterinary clinic can cost thousands of dollars to produce, but it is not that way with online video.

You can create the videos yourself with a cell phone that has a good camera, like the iPhone, or a simple video camera, or you can use any number of inexpensive software to create animated or slide-show videos.

Another choice is to hire a video production company to do it all for you, that way it ensures that it gets done properly and in a timely manner.

Perfectionism - perfectionism stops most people from trying to achieve anything great or worthwhile because as so many think "If I can't do it perfectly, I would rather not do it at all."

Nobody is perfect, and when potential clients watch your videos, they want to see a "real" human being, not some slick, perfect-looking, perfectly-spoken doctor.

Anyone who is wildly successful in their chosen career or profession had to start somewhere. The more you do, the more confidence you'll build.

Here are 2 tactics to help you get over perfectionism:

- **Start Small** - Don't set out to make the next Hollywood blockbuster video from the start. Do something small. How about recording a one minute video sharing a product review of one of the products you have for sale in your office? Then the focus isn't on you, you are just sharing your opinion on the pros and cons of a product. This can be a small way to get into video with something you already have planned.

- **Take Risks** -- No one has succeeded in anything without putting themselves out there. Risk is part of doing business. You will never know if something works if you don't do it.

The important fact to take away from this is to ignore your perfectionism and move forward with creating your first video. It doesn't have to be perfect, and it doesn't even have to be great. Getting started is half the battle.

****

Good is good enough - Mike Koenigs

****

3 reasons video may not work for you:

1. The obvious – you're just not doing it. Nothing works if you don't work it. To get the results, you must create videos that are interesting, relevant and provide value to your potential clients. Video works if you work it!

2. Your videos are boring – if there is no reason to be watching your video, or it is just too boring to get through, it is not going to work. Be yourself and do not be afraid to let your personality shine through so you can really connect with those potential clients. If it is bland, then it will simply go unnoticed

3. You are not optimizing them – you can't put them up on YouTube and expect people to just find your videos. You need the proper keywords, titles, descriptions and tags or you will be wasting your time

Video is simply a marketing tool...NOT a magic bullet!

9 Video Marketing Mistakes to Avoid

If you are going to put your time, energy and money into creating videos, you will want to avoid these next 9 mistakes so that you can have the best chance of success!

****

When you fail to make a plan, you plan to fail

****

Mistake #1 – No goal or intention for your video

Do not create a video unless you have a specific goal or intention for that video or you will have a tendency to ramble on without making any point, and will definitely lose a viewer's attention.

Mistake #2 – No call-to-action

Every video MUST have a call-to-action. You must let your viewers know what to do after watching the video, or nothing will happen. They will simply leave your video and go on to the next one.

Be sure to give specific direction, such as "For more information call our office at (555) 555-5555," "Visit our website," "Like us on Facebook," or "Subscribe to our channel."

Mistake #3 – Making your video too long

Keep your videos short, sweet and to the point. There are times when it is appropriate to create longer videos, but for most of the time, about 2 minutes or less is generally best.

Say what you need to say in order to get your message across and nothing more. The longer the video, the more people will click away from it.

Mistake #4 – Not sticking with one point

If you are creating a video about how to brush dog's teeth, just talk about how to brush a dog's teeth. Do not talk about how to clean their ears, or clip their nails, or talk about how to brush a cat's teeth. (wait, is that even possible??!)

Information overload in your videos will only confuse people, and confused people don't take action.

Mistake #5 – Not properly optimizing your video

As discussed in video marketing strategy #7, you need to use proper keywords, titles, descriptions and tags for your videos to give them the best chance of being found in the search results.

Mistake #6 – Expecting instant results

Video marketing is not a magic bullet. It takes time, consistency, dedication and a little patience to start seeing results, but it can have snowball effect after some time. The more video content you have online, the better the results you will have.

Mistake #7 – Thinking you need fancy, expensive equipment

Simply put – you don't. You don't need to shoot your videos in a studio with a tv-style video camera, a green screen background, a $500 microphone and professional lights all around you.

Yes, you want to have good lighting, and you want the sound of the video to be clear, so it is helpful to buy a microphone that you can plug into your phone or camera, but you don't need to spend a lot of money for this.

Just get started making your videos and then you can invest in more equipment if you want to.

Mistake #8 – Making boring videos

If your videos are boring, people will click away immediately. Do your best to be energetic, include humor if appropriate, and choose music that is upbeat.

Be careful not to speak in a boring, monotone voice. Be authentic, be "you" and let your personality shine!

Mistake #9 – Forgetting to share your videos

Once your video is uploaded to YouTube that is not the end. In fact, it's just the beginning!

Share your video everywhere you can – Facebook, LinkedIn, Twitter, Instagram, Pinterest, etc. And if your video is relevant and helpful, you might be pleasantly surprised to see others sharing your video with their friends.

Bonus Mistake #10 – Not making videos

Obviously, if you are not making videos, you will have ZERO results.

****

When it comes to effectively integrating video in your marketing, the best advice is this: don't be intimidated, start small and build from there

****

Why Online Video is the Future of Content Marketing

Without content, the internet would not exist. Content is the lifeblood of the internet, and it is the reason that we go online.

In earlier days, content consisted only of text on a page, which then morphed into using lots of flashy imagery on the page in an attempt to spruce it up.

Things have changed drastically in the last few years. We have now entered the online video age, and judging by what we have seen so far, it is likely that online video is the future.

The explosion in video popularity may come down to the fact that people spend hours watching television, movies and playing video games. Very few people want to pick up a book nowadays.

People really do not want to have to read through a lot of text when they can get all that they need in just a couple of minutes watching a video, and that is unlikely to change any time soon.

Your clients ARE online, searching for information, searching for answers to their questions, solutions to their problems, product reviews, reviews of businesses, and many other reasons.

Search engines know that this is the type of content that people want, and it is their job to serve up the content that is most in demand.

Using video as a content marketing method is absolutely perfect for local businesses because people are more inclined to watch videos than read, and video content is much more likely to convert viewers into clients.

Also, in this age of social media, more people are sharing content than ever before, and sharing textual content just isn't as much fun as sharing a great video with friends, family, and colleagues.

You hear about viral videos, but you never hear about viral articles!

If you have not started using video to market your veterinary clinic, it is definitely time to add it so that you can enhance what you are already doing.

It is important to keep in mind that video does not have to be sophisticated or elaborate to be effective. The key is to speak directly and openly to the viewers and make sure to add a call to action in each video.

At the end of the day, it's all about communication and relationships. Video is an ideal tool to create connections that help build that "know, like and trust".

Just go for it. You already have what it takes. You are already an expert. Nothing is stopping you but you.

****

The key is to just get started!

****

BONUS

Below is a video marketing checklist to give you a visual that you can look at when you are ready to start creating your videos. It is helpful even if you decide to hire a video production company.

Video Marketing Checklist

Who is my video is for?

_____

What is it I want to convey?

_____

- ❏ The type of video I am going to produce:
    - ❏ FAQs and SAQs
    - ❏ How To Videos
    - ❏ Client Testimonials
    - ❏ About Us Video
    - ❏ Home Page Video
    - ❏ Product Demos
    - ❏ Product Reviews

- ❏ Style of video:
    - ❏ "Talking Head" (me, live on camera)
    - ❏ Off Camera Interview style
    - ❏ Slide Show Video
    - ❏ Animated Video
- ❏ I have ensured my video does one of the following:
    - ❏ Helps
    - ❏ Teaches
    - ❏ Inspires
    - ❏ Entertains

- ❏ Makes people laugh or brightens their day
- ❏ I have made sure I:
    - ❏ Got my message across as briefly and clearly as possible
    - ❏ Removed all visual distractions from the area appearing on screen
    - ❏ Paid attention to lighting; ambient noise such as wind or traffic; sound
    - ❏ Edited out anything that doesn't directly enhance my message
    - ❏ Made sure background colors don't detract or distract
- ❏ I am using a:
    - ❏ smart phone
    - ❏ web camera
    - ❏ video production company

- ❏ I have planned my Video:
    - ❏ I have a goal for my video
    - ❏ I have a call to action for my video
    - ❏ I know the look and feel I want

- ❏ I know the type of video I'm going to create

- ❏ I have:
    - ❏ Uploaded my video to YouTube
    - ❏ Included relevant keywords in my Video Title and Description
    - ❏ Kept the length to 3:00 minutes or under
    - ❏ Embedded my Video on my blog
    - ❏ Shared my Video on Social Media
- ❏ I am doing the happy dance for completing and uploading my video!

What's Next?

Just go for it.

You already have what it takes.

You are already an expert.

Nothing is stopping you but you.

The key is to just get started!

Register This Book and Get

Free Updates and Free Videos

To get updates to this book and access to FREE informative videos that will show you how to attract new clients with videos, visit www.VeterinarianVideoMarketingBook.com, you can also text your email address to 1 (909) 570-1605 or scan this QR Code:

www.ingramcontent.com/pod-product-compliance
Lightning Source LLC
Chambersburg PA
CBHW070831180526
45168CB00002B/800